AF691339

Poems *from* Underground

Poems *from* Underground

On Depression, Faith, and Identity

JASON J. YODER

RESOURCE *Publications* • Eugene, Oregon

POEMS FROM UNDERGROUND
On Depression, Faith, and Identity

Copyright © 2026 Jason J. Yoder. All rights reserved. Except for brief quotations in critical publications or reviews, no part of this book may be reproduced in any manner without prior written permission from the publisher. Write: Permissions, Wipf and Stock Publishers, 199 W. 8th Ave., Suite 3, Eugene, OR 97401.

Resource Publications
An Imprint of Wipf and Stock Publishers
199 W. 8th Ave., Suite 3
Eugene, OR 97401

www.wipfandstock.com

PAPERBACK ISBN: 979-8-3852-8907-3
HARDCOVER ISBN: 979-8-3852-8908-0
EBOOK ISBN: 979-8-3852-8909-7

VERSION NUMBER 07/10/26
Quotation from Virginia Woolf, *Jacob's Room* used by permission of Harcourt Publisher.

He would go into Parliament and make fine speeches—but what use are fine speeches and Parliament, once you surrender an inch to the black waters?

—Virginia Woolf, *Jacob's Room*

Contents

Growing Up

When a boy
he wanted to be
a farmer
a truck driver
a mechanic
when he grew up.

Instead—
he grew up to be one
who practiced self-control
so that the thing within
would not swallow him whole
and become visible
to the outside world.

Days of His Life

Toddler on the floor, tugging at a dress,
in doting mother's gaze exulting;
a shining world is this tot's home.

(cloud of grayness flitting near the ground)

Lunch box with sandwich and fruit
and corn chips and cookies;
big yellow school bus enlarging the world.

(breeze of wistfulness cavorting with the soil)

Sun beaming down on summer's dream,
with trees and dog and lazy creek;
the world is tailor-made.

(instrument of rumination turning over the sod)

School on Sunday with friends all around,
learning to love and loving to learn;
God's in heaven, all is well in the world.

(seed of melancholia germinating in the dirt)

Cousins galore with uncles and aunts,
conversing, eating, playing—belonging;
a world responsive to his touch.

(stream of *Weltschmerz* coursing on the surface)

Storm and stress in youthful floundering,
boyhood now tucked into memory;
still, the world a gilded place to be.

(sorrow of time hovering above the land)

Tugged here and there as teen-time slips by,
forging a faith and seeking a work;
college commenced, the world is at his feet.

(weight of being brooding over the earth)

Shimmering days of his life;
surely, more enchanted days to come.

Stealthy implosion of world turns days into daze.

As he advanced toward adulthood,
depression advanced toward him.

Eastern Herald

This one lurched out of the east,
perceived by some as just shy of beast.
A sojourner—and to young eyes—a mystery,
lost lamb of Ammann, divorced from history.

Uncouth at the table and disheveled clothing,
sneaking a smoke—spawning a loathing.
A life is for loving, to be celebrated,
his presence, at best, was just tolerated.

O Cadillac, thou landlocked bird,
your proud flight evoking the absurd.
Wisp of Melchizedek, no beginning or end,
still aloft in mind's sky, the heavens to rend.

A nameless cry on a Sunday eve,
father and son bidding him leave.
Breath of eternity, whisper sublime,
this cry in the dark seared in my mind.

A woman with name of month of spring,
wed to the man—did the angels sing?
Wrestling with demons plundering joy,
bedeviled place from which to love a boy.

Sunday morn and gauntlet thrown down,
pilgrim on the doorstep—homeward bound.
Do I see it as privilege or do I see it as chore,
to sojourn a spell with the one at the door?

Stairway encounter between a man and a man,
frustrated dance enmeshed with the ban.
A question mark personified,
trail littered by some who tried.

Somewhere out there, perhaps alive, a mother,
sharing his blood—maybe sister and brother.
Stately name from the Old Testament given,
no doubt viewed as sunshine from heaven.

His tortured being made him easy sport,
for those whose pain more disguised—that sort.
A clouded mirror, in whom was seen,
unsettling vistas of what might have been.

He passed from life in a state young and old,
the depth of his torment left untold.
Alone in life, was he alone in death,
was anyone near when he drew a last breath?

Clearer now, than before, the trajectory of being:
here a little, there a little, through dark glass seeing.
Unlikely soil from which I grew,
ah, with anguished gladness I remember you.

Dawn

Dawning as gradually as adulthood
the knowing author put it down
with words that match my trek
such elegant corroboration
recognition breaking on the mind
like a ray of day-breaking sunshine
whisper-soft solace for one at home
with forlorn nocturnal stations:
verbalized dawn stroking the soul.

Depressive tendencies (severe)
written in what seems another life
earnestly and in olden cursive script
halting stabs to journal and clumsy
at sixty-five looking back through time
peering down on twenty-two-year-old
on whom it was dawning that
it had gradually dawned on him—
and it was the dawn of his future.

Sons of Menno

Good sons of Menno
known for working hard,
against idleness or
laziness also work to guard.

Good sons of Menno
build, fix, farm, and dig,
buying, selling too
some even make it big.

Good sons of Menno
can nurse and even teach,
work behind a desk and
run a store—some on Sunday preach.

Good sons of Menno
sweat and huff and puff,
until Sunday comes around
and then they say "enough."

But a good son of Menno
can one really be,
working out salvation
while writing poetry?

Father, Father

Three live wires on worn arm chair
in big house on old home place,
a black and white photograph:
May '64 caught in time and space.

Older brother on his right
and younger one on left side,
in husky, hairy fatherly arms
two rascals of Elmer S. abide.

Older son howls abandonedly
while face of other shyly beams,
and father in center, stoic smile—
'tis stuff of homemade dreams.

In my father's firm embrace
four years old, I am secure,
father, strong and steady
exuding love that will endure.

In my Father's firm embrace
ornery boy-man still finds rest,
and facing savage winds of life
knows he is safe—and doubly blest.

Normality

You might say
that you never knew:
I seemed so normal.

But normality can
be a tricky thing,
slipping through our fingers.

We tend to see what
we want to see,
wanting to see normality.

So often I thought,
just try harder,
then I can be normal.

So, the normal kept
showing its face
as I hid abnormality.

Hiding abnormality,
trying hard to make it,
became normality.

Thus, I did seem normal
and I can understand
that you never knew.

We all are a blend of
normal and abnormality;
when I see you
what exactly do *I* see?

Poems from Underground

Pressure building
for some six and forty years;
an outlet it is finding—
fueled by subterranean tears.

This tussle with depression
concealed so long from sight,
herein pushes upward
inching toward the light.

Might it help your point of view
if in these lines you found,
not the ramblings of a freak
but poems from underground?

John

You had so much life to live,
so much sparkle, love to give.

Leaving us one summer day,
why, oh why, did you not stay?

So many hearts broken—slain,
lying wounded on open plain.

Musing, if you had not gone,
how might now the lines be drawn.

Six and forty years after, you I find,
stalking still the chambers of my mind.

You left so quickly—such an end!
farewell cousin, buddy, friend.

Haunted

In year ten and nine
a bewildering brew
of vulnerability—
a drowning
a tipping point—
descent into destiny.

It just seemed
to have a way
of moving in
and taking over
when it first appeared
as uninvited guest.

Years and years on
the guest remains as embedded ghost
and if it were to leave—
what would become of solitary host?

Civil War

It is the day the Lord has made:
muted yet sincere rejoicing
fragile gladness whispering
points of light in inner space
warm hint of latent miracle.

Menacing weight of anxiety
patch of grayness levitating
fending off a chill of nausea
nihility somewhere stealing in:
nothing gnawing noiselessly.

This civil war within my being
invisible lines of battle drawn
back and forth the forces shift:
no exit from this battlefield
caught I am—no side will yield.

Disciples

Walking by the Galilee, so blue
two fishing brothers did he see,
without delay he called to them,
Come, cast in your lots with me.

Going on, behold, two more
mending nets, James and John,
and calling out he bid them
Come—and their hearts he won.

He came upon a sitting soul
all alone and coins collecting,
until he called to Matthew
and he heard, old way rejecting.

In another place a woman:
Lord, my daughter! Will you bother?
Seeing faith, he healed her
and, also claimed a mother.

Somewhere along the way
he came on Mary Magdalene,
calling her from bondage—
demons gone, life swept clean.

Women from all around
fell in step behind the man,
and who can tally up
the full number in that band?

He called to me one day
and every day he calls anew:
Your depression is no secret,
come, there is a place for you.

Interface

1

Why this malaise
whirring of uneasiness
pervading all my days?

Why this inner isolation
a nipping coolness
in tandem with negation?

Why this wandering in mist
on summit high
and below, cloudy bliss?

Why this time fixation
nearly omnipresent
bearing down with obduration?

Why this flirt with the absurd
as one looking down
like slow-circling bird?

2

Could it be that I—
in morass of existentialism
almost as much
as swamp of depression-ism?

Maybe too much Dostoevsky
too much of Camus
too much *Nausea*
and the Danish bloke, so blue.

Do not these two isms
cavort within one frame
(but making no mistake
they are not one and same)?

3

When desist from queries
and morbid analysis
from the inward look
and introspective paralysis?

4

Stop the infernal quest!
this the counsel
you may give:
yet same as telling
this romantic rascal
to give up—cease to live.

Tears in the Morning

Parked on the stairs
head in hands
wanting to disappear
fade from the scene
battling nameless dread
thought of trudging off to work
striking terror in the breast—
and weeping in despair.

Something wrong
something not right
in a twenty-nine-year-old
broken, facing breaking day
clock ticking toward doom
caught up in dreadful bind
heading to the gallows—
and weeping in despair.

When the going gets tough
strong men get going
instead of grinding to a halt
trembling in fear
stepping off the edge
melting down
grasping for a lifeline—
and weeping in despair.

It is not easy to be a
son
husband
father
provider
leader
man—
while weeping in despair.

Daily Bread

cup of coffee at mid-morn
soulful music plucking heart
completing irksome task
twinkle in wife's eyes
full tank and open road
warm bed on winter's night
big-eyed moon in eastern sky
peace from right thing done
grandson's burst of energy
through fingers pages slipping
surprised by praying power
pure blush of maid and young
to aid a wanderer in distress
swinging tail of faithful dog
stiff wind caressing cheeks
. . . whiffs of heaven's embrace.

simple daily pleasures
pall of cynicism
life-sustaining treasures
lure of nihilism

My God, my God . . .

The Scarlet Letter

For it to surface within God's flock,
I fear a fate unclear to me.

Not my goal to make a scene,
cause a stir or rock the boat;
seeking neither pity nor attention,
to curry kid-glove status—so remote.

Not craving special prayer,
or churchly counsel to descend;
good folks with good intentions,
therein a wounding can portend.

For it to surface within God's flock,
I fear a fate unclear to me:
perhaps in place of Hester's A,
stamped on my chest, a dreaded D.

103rd Psalm

Lure of crackling fire
glow of memory,
diamonds in the sky:
blessings pure of deity.

Gift of solitude
music in the wind,
fullness of a rose
strains of violin.

Cool at end of day
rocky mountain steep,
final page of book
giving in to sleep.

Young girl's dream
unruly clouds above,
faith's persistent push
joy of aging love.

Simple act of kindness
crack of splitting wood,
autumn morning crispness:
existence of the good.

Bless the Lord, O my soul,
heaven meeting earth,
life aglow with wonder—
a future seeking birth.

Something

Years floating by
time and again
asking self:
am I flawed?
what is wrong?
is not right?
this my plight.

Something
lurking round
to hold me back
keep me down
get me off track.

Silent assassin of
drive
career
advancement
opportunities
ambition
possibilities.

Then
something
showed its face
and I reckoned with
depression's terrible power:
sapping life of meaning,
draining gold of its gleam.

No fairy tale ending here
no grand victories to claim.
Still, a precious triumph—
something has a name.

First Interlude

But as constant as the beat of the heart, as sure as the rising of the sun in the morning, it remains. The darkness persists, pursuing me at all times and in all places . . . How attractive death appears at times.

—The author, from a journal entry, age 22

Shadow Land

Traces of failure in the blinding night,
disguised as victory in broad daylight.

Waves of despair—ocean wide, ocean deep—
lap the shore of the depths, too tired to weep.

Trapped from within and bound from without,
no cry breaches walls, whether whisper or shout.

'Tis hard not to wail, to whimper—to wonder;
flight from crazed wolf pack, a taste of its thunder.

Aye, my dear ones fiercely I love,
and I know I am loved, both below and above.

Yet, no exit looms up, no door is at hand,
so, this flawed wisp of being flows out into sand.

Dragon of darkness, ogre of day,
dance partners of pain, be gentle, I pray.

D1 and D2

Depression, denial—wrecking crew,
let us call them simply D1 and D2.

D2 aids and abets voracious D1,
enabling a sad life, beat and undone.

D1 looks for way to disguise its face,
by veiling visage D2 finds its place.

See, D1 freely can start to assail,
when D2 keeps one off its trail.

To get D1 or at least gain ground,
D2 must be pinned and well-bound.

Easier said than done, to master D2,
for hiding D1 is its mission to do.

So go after D2, fight the good fight,
then D1 will lose a bit of its bite.

Future Tens-ion

There is *no* future in depression.

There is no *future* in depression.

Beholden

Women—three, loving me.

Knowing me
yet still loving me.

How did they love me?
Let me count the ways:
rooting when I questioned
protecting when I flailed
waiting when I drifted off
carrying when I staggered
cheering when I triumphed
accepting when I self-loathed
believing when I doubted.

Bending the knee
to the God of Esther,
the God of Donna-Marie,
and the God of Naomi.

Mr. Shimerda's Descent

Meaning-full life in Bohemia
precious land of his birth
working to provide
nearby loyal comrades—
and a reason to play his violin.

Swept away by push and pull
to a life strange and new
on forlorn Nebraskan prairie—
with no reason to play his violin.

Unable to reinvent himself
a huge horizon shrunk his world
to a population of one.

Within that one, finally,
breathing was meaning-less.

Silently rested his violin.

Doing Time

Wearing down and
wearing out
carved out by loss on
loss—sucked dry.

What remains of bright
and curious lad
who once climbed trees
and sang to the sun?

Poking through time
adrift on time's current
downstream to where it goes
running on and running out.

No way out but way down
slow spiral to nothingness.

Washed up
and washed out.

Presence and absence
and absence ascending.

Last chance house
on high plains
still stands (and stands still):
stairs pining
rooms mourning
doors drooping
windows weeping
no echo of laughter finds a corner to brighten.

Survival mode—
but to what end?

On Loss

1

Who am I to go
where angels fear to tread?
let another muse instead:
still loss, it has grazed me
so I put words to my reality.

2

When a child's pet
hit on the road
sad boy or girl
hit too by grief,
by loss.

Jilted by love
young man crushed
by fair maid's no
grief runs its course,
with loss.

Career dreams fade
for one starry-eyed
left picking up pieces
grappling with grief,
and loss.

Midlife crisis looms
questions faced and
unsettling doubts, yes
there can be grief,
a sense of loss.

Aged parent passes on
aging child left behind
laden with emotion
tinged with grief,
for loss.

3

Loss of child's pet
not like loss of child
this we understand:
yet all loss is real and
matters to one who lost.

Grief-filled brush
with pain-laced loss
pierced by onward flow
we also understand:
'tis common to all.

4

Seems like melancholia
has deftly sharpened
my response to loss
like grinding wheel:
pointy and prickly too.

Loss is always there
discerned in daily hum:
lost opportunities
missed liveliness—
mist fading like a dream.

Mother dear, you
knew how tidings glum
could bring on a cloud

hovering over and
rippling through.

Depression's furtive turn
of steady grinding
over time and through,
a sense of losing out—
as the moments fly.

Loss and grief
and companion, sadness
by now a spider's web
of tangled mingling:
sorrow and depression.

Sense of loss now
interwoven in my being:
whether sorrow leads
to depression or
other way—I know not.

5

To write of loss
can make me sad
but in claiming
pointy, prickly part
of me—a nugget I find.

And, a trail of losing,
it might be kept in mind,
does not a loser make:
now and then—it is enough,
I find God's tracks in loss.

6

A curtain lifts,
a fleeting view of love I see
loss framed against eternity:
my God, you know loss as well—
and then the curtain fell.

The Wall

1

Through ticking time
of a halting dream
a wall discerning,
serpentine-like,
looming ahead and
compelling one
to find another way—
what more can I say?

2

The wall: made of depression-shaped blocks
and who knows what all else.

The wall: standing tall between
the present and the future.

The wall: timeless moments tumbling
into a lost and lonely lifetime.

The wall: caught in a convoluted dance
and dance partner's dark embrace.

The wall: diversion into detours
splattered with pain and love.

The wall: transparent barrier
hindering personal visibility.

3

The wall: just like that
the beast has turned on me—
I despise my poetry
and face the creeping misery.

Part 2 and Part 1

Part 2

Breakdown of heart on cold winter night:
flight for life and fight for life
body on fire and head exploding
shocked back into the land of the living.

Aspirin and
lisinopril and
atorvastatin and
clopidogrel and
metoprolol.

Meds to ward off another breakdown:
wanting to live
wanting to love, be loved
wanting to care for loved ones.
People "get" medication for the heart.

Part 1

Breakdown of the psyche—when?
too many times to count
too many shades to parse
veiled fight to stay in the land of the living.

Prozac and
venlafaxine.

Meds to ward off a living death:
wanting to live
wanting to love, be loved
wanting to care for loved ones.
People do not always "get" medication for the mind.

Cognitive Chaos

idiot loser losing mind
better off without me
fatally flawed a misfit
mistake disappear
never been born why try?
failure scream dummkopf
never amount to anything
nothing to show for my life
start driving never come back
do nothing right get in the way
mess up so stupid
nut case too much to take
punch something loser

Wandering in the wicked wasteland
of a diabolical internal dialogue.

So sorry, I am, for words hard to hear
(make them, you say, *make* them disappear).

It is true:
depression is more than feeling blue.

It has power to make one
say things to oneself
that one would never say
to someone else.

Prayer of a Phantom

Our Father, which art in heaven . . .

triggered by carnivals in the sky
watered by silky sand and dry

Beside melancholia,
if that were not enough,
there are these other traits—
foibles and stuff:
quirks and eccentricities
oddities and idiosyncrasies
blazing stars and bulls in poplar trees.

Bread this day
and forgiveness too
help for evil to eschew.

Did I come off the assembly line
without all my parts,
now going through life in fits and starts?

A passing phantom
neither circle nor square
where do I fit? (if anywhere).
Thank you, Lord, for being there.

At times things seem clear to me
as if approaching normality,
at times the pieces lay scattered . . .

Only you can prevent forest fires:
Only me?
Surely others bear responsibility too.

My life is a wreck
I am a mess:
fearful, withdrawn,
prone to obsess . . .

. . . and tethered to a Ferris wheel

Lord, this my ragged prayer, my plea:
that others might see Christ in me.

For thine is the kingdom . . .

Grounded

With sleek body
wings swept back
a plane is built to fly,
engines at full throttle
pointed heavenward
thrust into the sky.

It could feel as if
I was born to soar
spread my wings and fly,
but time and again
never leaving runway
and not knowing why.

Not to complain
make excuses
for staying earthbound,
but now knowing
that too much weight
kept me on the ground.

Monday Mourning

Wanting to go away
pull back from life,
yet knowing her love
the lifeline of my wife.

Thought of giving up
yielding to despair,
yet flitting in my mind
a distant mother's prayer.

No point in going on
it is too hard to cope,
yet their faces do appear
father's messengers of hope.

Burden to one and all
no more need to bother,
yet sensing I am held
and carried by my Father.

Blank wolf at door
wanting to fade away,
yet still trying to put
a crooked smile on this day.

Shades of Melancholy

on the surface floating
waters lapping
drifting through the days
gently straining

storm clouds gathering
waters stirring
floundering in the moment
fitfully treading

downward spiraling
waters covering
descending into darkness
invisibly drowning

Let It Be

1

Divine Spirit o'er water's face hovers
earth without form and void
the face of the deep, darkness covers.

Within and beyond this sacred mystery
incomparable Voice explodes
Let there be light—'twas pure creativity.

2

Together braided in earths depths, wild
eye of Deity peers faultlessly
secret works, and wondrous—a wee child.

Within and beyond the maternal womb
brilliant Will bursts forth
for diminutive creation, Let there be room.

3

In time and space, graciously immersed
the holy Wind still hovers
pristine energy, and lavishly disbursed.

Perplexed by brokenness, fears increase
word of eternal One breaks in:
you have I formed, Let there be peace.

Strangers

1

Hello, stranger,
have we met before?
I am a ghost of a man,
in search of a self—a core.

2

Why yes, stranger,
we have met before.
I am your dark shadow,
whom you seek to ignore.

3

So, we are strangers,
having met before.
Strangers for so long,
can we ease this tug of war?

Presence

Knowing and searching
when standing and sitting
never caught off guard
by thoughts and ways
of one so odd:
My God.

When lying down or
thinking strange thoughts
whether finding words
or drifting into worlds
where none hear it:
Your Spirit.

Losing the way in
the light of noon
and finding the path
by beams of the moon
a tinge of despair:
You are there.

Laboring to align
goodly design with
frame so frailly
fraught by visions this
world cannot afford:
O Lord.

Ravaged by beauty
beyond mortal expression
while bewildered with
malice aforethought
and other evil done:
Eternal One.

Searching and knowing
trying and seeing
roving through the
ways of one so weak
leading through the maze:
God of my days.

Limping through pain
savaged by the dark
struck down by the light
caught up in ecstasy
conception to senescence:
Presence!

Second Interlude

So often it can seem to me as if there is some flaw in my being that I can't identify and that seeks to undo me.

—The author, from an email to his parents, age 47

Existential Gravity

Newton's encounter with an apple
while sitting 'neath a tree,
a lesson learned about
a downward pull, called gravity.

Yoder's experience with a force
while eking out a destiny,
an insight gained about
a downward pull—melancholy.

Ferality

1

There once was a lad, eager and bright,
whose course devolved, sucked into night.

Questions swirl round and pile high,
what when where how who, especially why.

2

Where does one stop and the other begin?
A query unlike angels on head of a pin.

Temperament, constitution, personality,
inborn traits sketch in a hard reality.

Family of origin, experiences bad and good,
act to shape the contours of personhood.

Genetic makeup, I hear, does not seal destiny,
rather, hints at possibilities of vulnerability.

Not to be downplayed is the role of stress,
affecting one and all, more or less.

Brain chemistry, while hard to explicate,
one must reckon with, not underrate.

Interpersonal relationships, the I and Thou,
mold lives, in ways we know not fully how.

Obsessions and compulsions, fear, anxiety,
such, and others, here it is—comorbidity.

While determinism some choose to extol,
seems clear that choices made, too, play a role.

Contagious or not, the issue has loomed,
heredity, environment—are children doomed?

Treatment and prevention, wide open field,
some refractory, some helped, some healed.

No neat unriddling to the puzzle of disclosure,
there is risk in secrecy, risk in exposure.

Is it a separate entity, found out there,
that lurks in darkness, catching one unaware?

Or, might it be, this thing of dark design,
only takes form when inner pieces just so align?

Shirking the pull of depression to define me,
pushing beyond, beckoned by grander destiny.

Part of deity in cosmic drama, open to debate,
is better alternative (says I) than casting all to fate.

Wrestling with Jacob's God, through the night,
limping at break of day by faith, not sight.

3

A restive poetic offering might be extended,
but for sake of you, kind reader, will be ended.

Accounting for the thereness of depression,
such exceeds my powers of expression.

Yet, I will never stop in the quest to know,
why melancholia has touched me so.

Poetic License

The other day
(in my imagination)
pulled over was I
by poetry police,
causing consternation.

Do you have license
poetry to write?
the officer asked
with grave tone,
as I concealed my fright.

Not clear to me
if one I had obtained,
clumsy sputtering
red-faced too,
shaking—feeling drained.

Said officer let me go
with warning stern,
to make sure the
poetry measured up,
but I, the standard, did not discern.

Treading lightly now,
no failure to want,
fearing that my penalty
could be a custom license plate:
INCOM-POET-ENT.

Morning

One of those mornings
too tired to fight
too tired to care
nothing seems right.

One of those mornings
is hard to think
hard to talk
horizons shrink.

One of those mornings
life a bad dream
if strength enough
I would scream.

One of those mornings
try to pray
lift up my eyes
to a God far away.

One of those mornings
hard to explain
look at me
it might be plain.

One of those mornings
I do not like me
let me sit, close eyes
just let me be.

One of those mornings
ride the wave
stay alive
pretend to be brave.

One of those mornings
the worst will pass
just like before
until next time, alas.

One of those mornings
the sky is blue—
and I am too.

Something About Nothing

Easier it would be, I reckon,
to say nothing about something
than to say something about nothing.

A clever thief, I know,
to subtly tap the vital substance
and leave behind a forlorn void.

Dream no more, I languish,
for struck down by furtive foe
they mangled lay on field of battle.

Taking, not giving, I tremble,
essential juices diminished
by that which feeds on nothing.

Lusting after nothingness, I fear,
seducing words and will
and whorishly pursuing the future.

Against its icy grasp, I stand,
compelled by slender cords of love
to say something about nothing.

Who Sinned?

That day while on the move,
a man born blind was seen;
questions rose and swirled within
those trainees of the Nazarene.

Teacher, someone sinned somewhere,
there is no doubt;
to cause such a condition
there is sin to be found, dug out.

It must be, it seems,
that the parents are to blame;
maybe the man himself
has hidden sin—it is all the same.

Surely, Rabbi, this is so,
a solution cannot be other;
the blind one has transgressed
or else his father and his mother.

His answer caught them by surprise,
their tradition overturned;
the teacher taught his pupils then
a lesson hard to learn.

You are blind, said he,
to God and to his ways;
there is goodness now at work
in this one blind for all his days.

So, then and there,
one blind first saw daylight;
while those curious students
first came to see aright.

Confession

Trusting in God and
laboring under troubled skies.
Some would say that real faith
should make for sunny days.

But is faith whispered
at dark midnight
necessarily less virile
than faith blazoned at midday?

Confessing that God
has been part of my story,
that God has not taken it away—
and holding on for dear life.

Family Tree

Giving thanks to God
for such a lineage;
grateful for my kin
and a faith-laced heritage.

In the clan, I know of some
who have plodded arduously;
yet how many more—
groaning imperceptibly?

Disquieted minds
among the quiet in the land;
facing inner demons
and doing the best they can.

How many of my relatives
on branches perched so silently?
How many might I find
if I would shake the family tree?

After All

When it presses in
the world
is so restricted,
but this is the
view for one afflicted.

When it presses down
the horizon
draws so near,
but this is the
sense, so crystal clear.

When it presses round
the lungs
they gasp for breath,
for, after all,
depression is a living death.

Miss Dickinson's Fall

I

Perceived a funeral, she
unfolding in her brain,
mourners moving round,
clutching still to sense in vain.

Mourners took their places
a service began to sound,
dragging and percussive
senseless mayhem to redound.

Burial box was lifted up
o'er her being grating,
with lifeless leaden boots
then sickly sound of desiccating.

Assailed by cosmic din
no place to go—to hide,
forlorn and ruined, she
with primal terror did abide.

Then reason torn asunder
down and down she fell,
escorted by the dark:
where ending, none can tell.

2

I cannot say for sure
what this poet did describe,
but seems to me, she
depression's poison did imbibe.

What Might Have Been

One hollowed out moment
gives way to another with
moments turning into years—
becoming a shell of a man
whimpering into the wind.

I wonder if some
see it in my eyes,
looking hard into
the abyss within,
discerning the form
of a shell of a man
whimpering into the wind.

I will never know
what might have been
if depression had not been:
I only know what is.

Lord, loose the chains of "what if"
so that I can give you "what is."

Trusting that you can do more
with a shell and a whimper
than with all my barren what ifs.

A Mother's Gift

She called it for what it was
prepared to see it as illness
unwilling to neatly collapse it
into the amorphous realm of the spiritual.
(Knowing how tender my heart was toward God.)

She affirmed the way I tried to
soldier on—as believer, husband,
father, leader—compensating for
the limp as best I could.
(Seeing how hard I tried to survive.)

She loved me as one hobbled by frailty
fleshing out her love through prayer
a maternal bond time and distance
could not weaken or sever.
(Intuiting how fragile her boy really was.)

The gift of a mother,
a gift like no other.

Face to Face

1

One thing it is to see it in myself,
to see it start to suck me dry,
taking breath of life away,
leaving me too dead to cry.

A difference there is when
contained and tucked within,
when the vital spark is lost,
one drifts amid a silent din.

Better, a little (viewed perversely),
when the pain, it bears my name,
and the eyes lose twinkle,
giving way to grayish flame.

Easier it seems, at least a bit,
to bear extinction of life force,
pushing ahead, woodenly,
with no purpose, no recourse.

2

But not the same, when seeing
it in another—grim winds wild—
seeing it in another face when
said visage is that of one's own child.

Looking Both Ways

Depression is being sixty,
looking back and wondering
what you have to show for
the last forty years.

Depression is being sixty,
looking ahead and wondering
how you will get through
the next twenty years.

Depression is being sixty-two,
looking ahead and wondering
if you even want to get through
the next twenty years.

Pretty Good

If my wife were to ask me today
how things stood,
without too much thought I could say
pretty good.

You might snort about this little thing—
you could,
but I give thanks to the Lord above
for pretty good.

What Do You Do?

I

Happening every now and then,
not long after How are you?
a question to make me squirm,
the simple query, What do you do?

No doubt it comes innocently,
to help a conversation flow;
mere curiosity no doubt,
an inquiry so harmless—apropos.

Finding ways to muddle through,
paste together a kind of résumé;
sputtering on as best I can,
seizing on some words to say.

'Tis clear they want to know
what I do to make ends meet;
how providing for the family
and keep from living on the street.

If only I could say a teacher
or a carpenter, a salesman too,
electrician, trucker, counselor,
or bookseller—this is what I do.

All these I have done, and more—
business owner, landlord, handyman;
yet hard it is to neatly say,
This I do and This I am.

2

With formal training to be
a worker in the church—pastor;
long years I labored
for such a trade to master.

Yet in the circles which I roam,
one does not pastor for a living;
rather, one makes a living to
lead a church—expected self-giving.

So, in the circles where I move,
it does not pay to lead a church;
thus caught, hard-pressed too,
to find the place for which I search.

3

Coursing through this narrative,
a melancholic trail of tears;
silent stalker of hopes and dreams,
ghastly beast feasting on my years.

It seems this ragged soul,
by depression flogged and flayed;
so beaten down, beaten up,
no future waits for me (I am afraid).

4

So, when asked, What do I do?
the question I must face;
groping for the words
to describe my work-world place.

But the deeper question lurks,
menacingly, concealed from sight:
What do I do, but struggle
to keep from slipping into night?

Excuse Me, Please

This poor excuse for a poem
is kind of like my life:
It is going nowhere.

Distant Mind

Ruminating on how depression
makes one feel out of place,
caught in a space warp of
detachment others do not face.

Lost in melancholic space
looking down on world unreal,
floating in another realm
and turning, turning goes the wheel.

Writing a poem about a
Plathian literary scene:
Ms. Greenwood and a book
enveloped in otherworldly sheen.

Third Interlude

Depression—and assorted goblins caught up in its gravitational field—has had considerable success in undoing this ontological blip on the cosmic radar that signifies my life.

—The author, about age 65

Almost 66

Facing drawn-out pain
on twisted journey:
inclined to cringe, to cower.
Surveying riddled years
through depressive prism,
behold! explanatory power.

Reviewing inner space
swept by swirling,
stinging winds, devouring.
Embracing that prism—
ripening heads of grain
in golden fields—empowering.

Portrait of a Clown

Paint sticks to the wall
as the brush goes up and down,
obeying silent orders
of an aging painting clown.

From can onto the brush
then onto wall, looming,
this my lot today,
back and forth, unassuming.

The brush keeps moving
and, too, my restless mind;
roaming to and fro,
melancholically inclined.

From somewhere deep within—
an urge to yield, to cry:
my soul is weeping
even though my eyes are dry.

Paint sticks to the wall
as my life goes up and down,
in doleful brushing strokes
of a weeping painting clown.

Impact

As minutes
depression
turn into hours
depression
and hours
depression
turn into days
depression
and days
depression
turn into months
depression
and months
depression
turn into years
depression
and years
depression
turn into decades
depression
and decades
depression
turn into a lifetime . . .

Who can rightly reckon up the devastation
wrought by this shifty foe—the discombobulation?

Writing

Battling to stay engaged with life—
vitality waning
lethargy arising
dull brain laboring
darkness pressing in
to go far away longing
talking a chore seeming,
and fighting back despair.

It can help to stay engaged
with words on page, a battle waged.

Complex Legacy

1

All my life she lived far away,
visits were short, we could not stay.

Reserved and shy, exceedingly kind,
for growing boy, sweet smile did find.

Partner in marriage, she never found,
no difference to me, wed or unbound.

Her love for the Lord, pure and sincere,
she treasured the Bible, held her faith dear.

Family nearby, a church family too,
resolved to live right, all sin to eschew.

2

Perhaps there were earlier clues of decline,
noted by others, with perspective not mine.

I know that at twenty and five years of age,
toll of friend's death, distress did presage.

Depression took hold, not going away,
heedlessly staying, to the last troubled day.

Then psychosis came on, came into view,
doubled her anguish, my heart breaks anew.

3

Boy became man, filled up with years,
beholding her journey, long trail of tears.

She never reached sixty, still five years shy,
no husband, no children, stood guard nearby.

I know many labored, to help ease the load,
stayed with, prayed for, blessing bestowed.

4

Close to death, in a dream viewed a river,
Jesus beckoned to cross, peace to deliver.

Whether dream, hallucination, delusion,
such a prospect of bliss, stirred up confusion.

Death near at hand, Bible open close by,
in posture of kneeling, whispered last cry.

5

With self assisting, from this life she passed,
in a way to perplex, leave the living aghast.

Most gentle creature, good willing to all,
harming another, would disturb and appall.

Something broke within, down fell night,
have mercy Lord—her mind—it was not right.

6

Dear loved aunt, flesh and blood, I weep,
entrusting to Jesus, your soul to keep.

Stigmatization

Do you have time for
a self-examination?

Does the idea of medication
present a complication
cause hesitation
affect valuation
arouse consternation
prompt self-congratulation
stir up indignation
engender condemnation?

Can you see why some who suffer
hold back information?

Faithful

What would happen if
I stopped my medication?
After years of being on it
what would be the sensation?

There is the wish
things go on as before:
more even keeled
fewer lows
greater drive
less grouch.
There is the wish . . .

Places not to go,
this is a place like that.
Too well 'tis known
what would come to pass:
time elapsing
seems all is well
then—mad clockwork:
slipping, sliding,
going down.

By hard way
I have learned
what med-less-ness
will do to me.

God-lovers perhaps wince
troubled by these words
disturbed by hard reality:
more Scripture, praying,
more faith, churchgoing,
more zeal, fervor true

cannot do
what meds
can do.

Even harder to digest
may be the thought:
being faithful with my meds
can help me
be more faithful to my God.

When something works
one keeps on doing it.

I will keep on doing
what keeps on working.

Whom Shall I Fear?

1

Fearing self-disclosure, for some
no doubt, will look askance,
though some days thinking
it is worth the risk, the chance.

Letting the dark secret out
will change my world, 'tis true,
but keeping it to myself
will have consequences, too.

2

What do I really fear
in disclosing to the world,
the secrets of the heart in
lines from underground unfurled?

Seen as morally deficient
or defective or weak-kneed,
maybe lacking manliness—
these fears my mind can breed.

More is the lurking fear
that some will sniff, ignore,
quietly my words dismiss
and condescendingly endure.

Most of all, there is fear
of a gaping disconnect,
from blank gazes in whom
no connection I can detect.

3

Yet, I muse, the faithful One
burrows through my story,
still wanting more to do
in me, and for God's glory.

4

In the end, I face the fear
and reckon with the cost:
these *are* my poems, and
hiding them, what will be lost?

The light and my salvation,
stronghold of my being:
if this be so, and it is so,
then I a coward am by fleeing.

Summation

If I had but one sentence to make a case:
Depression is a lonely place.

Declaration of Independence

A mistake it would appear to be,
linking identity with familiarity.

It is true, depression I have known;
but I declare, has not made me its own.

I am me and depression is an it;
though so tied together, it is separate.

So ends a little poem on identity:
I am me and it—it is a foreign entity.

Ineffable

Internal clock keeps ticking.

Supercharged consciousness of self
and of self's silent
and relentless
diminishment.

Haunting sense of loss,
of unfulfilled potential,
of life slipping . . . slipping away.

Background buzz of
immense longing,
nameless sorrow,
breaking the heart
like fragrance of new-mown hay.

Danger Zone

Finding it hard these days
to care much about anything,
feeling like the flame of life
is burning down, burning lower:
body tired, mind moving slower.

Finding it hard these days
to sit and drink in a book,
listen to favored music or
write some lines of poetry:
subject to a kind of entropy.

Finding it hard these days
to give a reason to be
(why finish this poem?):
a waning drama, now enacting,
this my world, dully contracting.

Finding it hard these days
to reach out to another
(bother no one, this my tack):
knowing, in jousting alone,
I have entered a danger zone.

Turning It Over

If it is hidden
is it also
a thing forbidden?

If it is hiding
is it also
in obscurity forever
to remain—
in mist abiding?

Turning it over
in my mind
like a piece of wood
turning over
in a lathe,
but not knowing
what will come forth.

Hearken, esoteric alchemy:
mist turned into mystery.

So, it is hidden
and, in a sense, forbidden.

Hidden knowledge, let me now its fruit to try!
yet, if you know it, then its mystery you do deny.

Turning it over
in my mind
like a piece of wood,
flecks of gold to find.

Knowing that the
knowledge it will never
fully show itself to me,
because hidden
and forbidden
it must always be.

Turning it,
turning it over,
turning it over all I can . . .
and knowing
I am a sick and wicked man.

Elusion

Northward driving late afternoon
day advancing toward its twilight
grand sky in mountain valley high
touch of pity for cattle braving cold
heater taking edge off chill in cab
old friend this truck homeward bound.

Saw-toothed mountains to the west
silhouetted against the frigid sky
clouds catching fire from hidden ball
fetching light of day to it as it runs
patches of rose-red, muted orange,
shades of color too fine to name
mingle with complex shifting shapes
of cloudy mist against snow-white
mounts with peaks jutting skyward
draws and ridges and crevices.

Like that, the scene luster loses
as darkness keeps on dawning
no way to freeze that frozen
sight of glory except in frail
mind's eye—grasping for words.

'Tis almost as if that wintery
western wilderness wonderland
in the sky and on the mountains
gives a fleeting flick of a long
life lived, and living still now
full of longing love joy loss
mourning beauty sorrow, all
compressed in the twinkling
of an eye within a vista in that
awful one and only moment.

Tears of Light

Stumble ye, therefore,
for the prodigals of righteousness
have returned;
enigmatic words from
a growing seed of promise
coming forth, from whom learned?

Youngest daughter, you
no longer are a girl so little
now a woman—grown;
effusing gentleness
light bubbling up
softly making presence known.

Mind of yours, darting here
darting there like
dancing strains of violin—baroque;
not caught off guard that
caught in mental shadows
you saw father—breaking, broke.

Dear child of mine, I
in this poem responding
weeping at your heart—so tender;
shifting shadows gray
not will the light dispel:
this to you, with love—I render.

Far Away

1

Somewhere along the winding path
was it lost and fell away,
or might it already have been missing
on that existential break of day?

Ah, loner in search of key,
free spirit looking for a clue,
restlessness cloaked in flesh,
union seeking with Spirit true.

No escape from primal tremble,
no respite from experience, raw,
relentless tug for something more—
hearken or withdraw?

Finding place in cosmic puzzle:
why the task so full of pain?
trapped in a life-sized riddle,
hard to convey, explain.

Is it this melancholia
or the way was made,
did some trauma mark me
or true calling did I evade?

2

Far away the music plays
against the questions of my days,
beckons softly, does entreat
to sing a song so full, so sweet.

Belonging

Speck of existence
flesh-blood-spirit:
why a clod of earth
God-image to inherit?

Enigma in a riddle
in a puzzle in a mystery:
single grain of sand
fleeting flake of frailty.

Wisp of human being
just an earthly clod—
yet taking heart:
I belong to God.

Notes on Selected Poems

Notes are intended to give credit where credit is due and, also, to provide some background information that can help the reader to better understand selected poems.

Epigraph

Virginia Woolf, *Jacob's Room* and *The Waves* (New York: Harcourt, Brace and World, Harvest Book, n.d.), 139.

Growing Up

My mother helped me to understand this matter of self-control (in relation to depression) when she wrote the following in an email in 2007: "You, Jason, I believe, work very hard at controlling it. You have a lot of self discipline [sic]. There's now [she means "no"] doubt in my mind concerning this."

Days of His Life

"God's in heaven, all is well in the world." This is a paraphrase of the lines in *Pippa's Song*, by Robert Browning (from his verse play, *Pippa Passes*): "God's in His heaven— / All's right with the world!"

Eastern Herald

Written around 2007, this poem represents an effort to interpret the life and death of a man who dealt with mental illness throughout much of his life. His journey brushed up against mine as I grew up.

Jakob Ammann was a Mennonite elder who became involved in a dispute among Mennonites in the last decade of the seventeenth century in Europe. Those associated with Ammann eventually became known as Amish.

Dawn

It is Andrew Solomon who writes, "Depression dawns as gradually as adulthood" (*The Noonday Demon: An Atlas of Depression*, New York: Scribner, 2001, 46).

In a journal entry, dated November 29, 1981, I refer to my "severe depressive tendencies."

Sons of Menno

Menno Simons (1496–1561) was an influential leader in the newly-birthed Anabaptist movement in Europe. His name became attached to some of the adherents of Anabaptism and it stuck—Mennonites.

The allusion in the last stanza is from Philippians 2:12.

Poems from Underground

The title and last phrase of this poem allude to Fyodor Dostoevsky's novel, *Notes from Underground.*

John

John drowned on June 27, 1979 at the age of nineteen while taking part in a church youth group outing.

Disciples

Background Scripture in this poem includes Matthew 4:18–22; Matthew 9:9; Matthew 15:21–28; Mark 16:9; and Mark 15:40–41.

Interface

The imagery in the third stanza is influenced by *The Wanderer Above the Sea of Fog*, a painting by Caspar David Friedrich (1818).

Nausea is the title of a novel written by Jean-Paul Sartre, first published in 1938.

"The Danish bloke" refers to Søren Kierkegaard.

Something

In the fourth stanza, I have been influenced by Jonathan Sadowsky when he writes of depression's super power: ". . . few maladies match depression's super power: to drain life of value, to turn what was golden into mud" (*The Empire of Depression: A New History*, Medford, MA: Polity, 2021, ix).

D1 and D2

The designation of depression and denial as D1 and D2 owes something to the mischievous Thing One and Thing Two of Dr. Suess notoriety.

Beholden

Esther is my mother's name. Donna-Marie, my first wife, died in 1993. I married Naomi in 1997.

Mr. Shimerda's Descent

Mr. Shimerda is the father of Ántonia in *My Ántonia*, by Willa Cather. To the best of my knowledge, Cather nowhere uses the term *depression* in relation to this man, but it is clear to me that he is severely depressed.

Doing Time

The reference to absence and presence in the sixth stanza draws on Peter D. Kramer: "The contrast between a patient depressed and a patient recovered is the contrast between absence and presence" (*Against Depression*, New York: Viking Penguin, 2005; Penguin, 2006, 13).

Last Chance is a small town in Colorado, situated east of Denver. Not far from the town is an old house that I have been observing over the years while driving through the area.

On Loss

Concerning the third stanza in part four of this poem, my mother wrote the following to me in an email dated June 8, 2007: "I have noticed news of tragedies weigh heavily on you. Years ago the separation of ________ daughter and husband was hard on you, as was John's death. You are aware of this, I am certain, and so need to work very hard to to [sic] keep a healthy sanity . . ."

Shades of Melancholy

One of my daughters came across information from an unidentified source describing three levels of depressive severity: floating on water, treading water, drowning in water.

Let It Be

This poem draws on Genesis 1:2–3 and Psalm 139:13–16.

Presence

This poem is my rendition of Psalm 139.

Ferality

In relation to genes and destiny, I have been influenced by chapter 10 of Daniel Goleman's study, *Social Intelligence: The New Science of Human Relationships* (New York: Bantam, 2006).

The reference to I-Thou is from Martin Buber's *I and Thou*.

The story of Jacob wrestling with God can be found in Genesis 32:22–32.

Something About Nothing

This poem owes some of its inspiration to two lines in *Practicalities*, by Marguerite Duras, *The Lover*, *Wartime Notebooks*, *Practicalities*

(Everyman's Library, 380, New York: Alfred A. Knopf, 2018), 348: "The only alternative is to say nothing. But that can't be written down." Duras is not dealing with depression in this context, but her remarks helped something to click concerning the challenge I have faced in writing about depression.

Who Sinned?

This poem is based on the first part of the account of Jesus healing a man born blind, as found in John 9.

Miss Dickinson's Fall

This is my recasting and interpretation of Emily Dickinson's poem, *I felt a Funeral, in my Brain.*

A Mother's Gift

Written in 2024, ten days before my mother's ninety-eighth birthday.

Distant Mind

Sylvia Plath portrays her main character in *The Bell Jar*, Esther Greenwood, as having a "distanced mind," looking on as she tries to begin a novel at her mother's house. See Sylvia Plath, *The Bell Jar* (Harper and Row, 1971; reprint, New York: Harper Perennial Modern Classics, 2005), 120.

Faithful

There is an allusion in this poem to information from Robert M. Sapolsky: Somewhere around the fourth episode of depression, "a mad clockwork takes over . . ." That is, subsequent episodes seem to be unrelated to stress triggers, like the first three or so (*Why Zebras Don't Get Ulcers*, 3rd ed., W. H. Freeman, 1994; New York: Henry Holt, Owl, 2004, 292).

Whom Shall I Fear?

This poem is influenced by Psalm 27, especially verse one.

Turning It Over

At the end of a lecture on depression by psychologist James Hillman, an audience member asked him to define the illness. Hillman became pensive and uncertain. He removed his glasses, rubbed his eyes, and dropped his chin into his hand. He looked over the heads of the audience and out the window. Finally, after clearing his throat, he responded: "Depression is hidden knowledge." See Jeffery Smith, *Where the Roots Reach for Water: A Personal and Natural History of Melancholia* (New York: North Point, 1999), 113.

The last line of the poem is my paraphrase of the opening words of Fyodor Dostoevsky's novel, *Notes from Underground* (translated by Richard Pevear and Larissa Volokhonsky, Everyman's Library, 271, New York: Alfred A. Knopf, 2004).

Tears of Light

My youngest daughter wrote the following, excerpted from a Father's Day letter she gave to me: "Thankyou [sic] for keeping the lights on, Dad. I see you living with the mental shadows, but you haven't let them have the final say."

www.ingramcontent.com/pod-product-compliance
Lightning Source LLC
LaVergne TN
LVHW022109200926
848481LV00003B/1130
* 9 7 9 8 3 8 5 2 8 9 0 7 3 *